Stock The
REAL FOOD
Pantry

Disclaimer

I am not a health care professional. I am a mom who believes that we are on the correct path for providing nutrient-dense, nourishing foods. You should do your own research and come to your own conclusions for your health care and nutrition along with consulting a health care professional. I highly recommend contacting the Chapter Leader of your local Weston A. Price Foundation and ask about a list of health care providers.

Copyright © 2013/2018/2020 Millie Copper

ISBN-13: 978-1-7327482-2-4

All Rights Reserved

Material is not to be copied, shared, or republished without prior written consent of the author. All methods/formulas are original or noted as inspired/adapted. Please visit HomespunOasis.com for other great ideas on how to nourish your family while on a budget.

Table of Contents

The Pantry Principle and More 1

Meet the Pantry 9

Building a Real Food Pantry 11

Before You Begin 13

Water 22

Heat and Eat 24

Beans & Legumes 29

Concentrate on Fats 38

Grains and Grain Alternatives 41

Seasonings and Spices 47

Preserved Foods 49

Sweeteners 54

Nuts and Seeds 57

Dairy and Dairy Substitutes 58

Miscellaneous 60

Focus on the Freezer 61

Preparing Food 65

Beyond the Pantry 67

Budget Thoughts 80

More From Millie Copper 89

Resources 91

Meet the Author 95

The Pantry Principle and More

The Pantry Principle is a phrase I first discovered in *The Complete Tightwad Gazette* by Amy Dacyczyn. According to this book, the basic principle is to stockpile your pantry with food purchased at the lowest possible price. Every time you shop, your only purpose is to replenish the pantry, not to buy specific ingredients to prepare specific meals.

Amy (I call her Amy because I've read her book so many times that I almost feel I know her) makes a point of saying that many people do this, but not to the extent that produces the largest cost savings.

Off and on for several years, we've followed the pantry principle. I love having a good supply of basic items on hand. It makes it so much easier for me to be able to plan our meals. I always shop our pantry before shopping other sources.

When we first started filling our pantry, we focused on items we could get dirt cheap. I'd scour the sales flyer and buy the "loss leader" items, thinking I was getting a great deal. Ten boxes of rice with seasonings for a dollar. Boxes of cake mix, muffins, and the like all went in my pantry. When

I found a good deal on things, I'd buy as many as were allowed or as my budget would let me.

I put together a price book, which helped me determine when I was getting something for a great price. I also used it to keep track of when things went on sale. All of this was very helpful with stocking the pantry.

I was very comfortable with using the pantry principle, and I planned our meals based on what we had on hand. Then I'd make a shopping list to pick up any other needed items, such as fresh produce or the occasional specialty ingredient.

Then, one day, I read an article about someone who took their pantry to a whole new level—way beyond anything I knew. That was when I was introduced to food storage.

I found the concept of food storage to be very interesting. I started researching food storage but didn't spend too much time on it. So much of the information that I found led me to believe food storage was the idea of buying a large amount of food (most places recommend a year supply) and storing it away until some major disaster happened and it was needed.

I have to admit, that didn't appeal to me at all. The recommended items to store weren't foods I was familiar with. I had no idea how to even cook most of the things! I put the idea of food storage out of my head and happily continued stocking my pantry. After all, while we couldn't "survive" on our pantry, we did have many weeks of food available to us. Yep, those many boxes of rice mix would get a little old, but I didn't worry about that.

In December of 2007, we had a wake-up call.

We lived in the Pacific Northwest when the Great Coastal Gale hit. On Sunday, the electricity went out. Monday morning, my husband left for work and returned about ten minutes later. Every road between our house and the highway was blocked by fallen trees. The wind was blowing something awful, but we didn't know it was blowing as bad as it was due to the location of our house.

We lived on the edge of a forest, and the number of downed trees was incredible. And with the wind still blowing and trees still falling, it was too dangerous to try to move the trees so Joe could go to work.

To top it off, the phones didn't work. Landlines and cell phones were both gone. We had a wind-up radio, but the local radio station wasn't transmitting. No power, no phone, no news, and no way out was an interesting place to be.

The following day, the wind had subsided, and after working with the chainsaw-carrying neighbors, we were able to get to the highway.

Town was seventeen miles west. None of the neighbors had been into town, and no one really knew what was going on. Both Joe and I wanted to check in with our employers since the phones were still out. My work was on the way to town, and Joe's was in town. The highway to town was covered in debris but passable.

Town was a disaster. Many, many shop windows had been blown out. There was no power. No gas stations were open. There was a grocery store open, accepting cash only and escorting people to a specially stocked area with a flashlight. Restaurants were closed. The banks were closed. (The next day, our bank reopened—sort of—and people could take out only $100 until the power came back on.) Plus, it was the beginning of the month and many people, including us, were expecting paychecks. Most paychecks are made in a computer, and without power, paychecks couldn't be easily figured and printed. And without the banks open, money couldn't be retrieved from those paychecks. It really was quite a mess.

The power started coming back on, the phones once again worked, and things started to reopen. At home, our power came back on Friday.

Things were starting to get back to normal when we had a setback. Due to the storm, a hillside gave way on one of the main roads into our town. That mudslide closed the road for several weeks. There was a noticeable drop in the restocking of depleted supplies while the road was closed.

Our event could've been worse as far as disasters go. There was loss of life, and our county was declared a disaster area, so it was bad enough. Major earthquakes, tsunami, tornadoes, and hurricanes happen often. I'm sure we're all familiar with Hurricane Katrina and other, more recent hurricanes.

Because of our food on hand, we weren't affected by the short-term power outage and lack of shopping. But we did notice that we didn't have a very good variety. I was wrong about enjoying those boxes of rice for any amount of time.

We were also fortunate to have water while the power was out. A town down the road from us was not so fortunate. The wind had knocked over a tree and taken out something important that made the water arrive at people's homes.

They were out of water for several days before the repairs were made.

After the storm, I started searching out more information on food storage. While we weren't really affected by the few days of power outage, another few weeks of no power and we would've worried about our food supply. Plus, our choices would become quite limited. Storms of that magnitude weren't common in our area, but the fact that it did happen was a huge wake-up call.

I started learning about food storage and sharing what I learned with my husband. To be quite honest, Joe was not 100 percent on board, but he said if I thought it was a good idea then to go ahead. That was before our real food journey had started, so my pantry stocking consisted of the standard items recommended by "survival" websites: shortening, lots of canned goods, and other similar items. I did get a small amount of whole wheat after Joe gifted me with a crank grain grinder, but that was the closest to a whole food item we had in our pantry. We built our pantry fairly well, to a point where we'd be good for a couple of months. Then things changed for us, and we moved. We stopped buying food and started eating what we had. By the time we settled in Wyoming, our stocked-up food was gone, and we were beginning our real food journey.

It took us a while to rebuild our pantry. Our money was tight, but we tried to put a few dollars toward extra things each month.

My big hang up was, what should we put in our pantry now that we eat real food?

By definition, real food is fresh food. It spoils. It took me a good year to get a handle on exactly *what* we wanted to store in our real food pantry.

Like before, Joe was okay with the idea but not overly excited. He agreed that buying things in bulk at a low price made good financial sense. He agreed that having a well-stocked pantry with food on hand would cut down on trips to town. He agreed that our Wyoming weather could make driving to town difficult some days—we've had snow drifts in our yard that were so high I was unable to get the car out for days. But he cautioned me not to "go nuts." He didn't want me buying so much food that it'd go bad before we could use it. We decided to build up three months' worth of food, plus a little more during the winter. That seemed like a reasonable amount that we could easily store and use.

Our real, whole, traditional foods diet focuses on consuming the highest quality ingredients that our budget allows. This often means we purchase these items from as close to the source as possible. Our beef comes from local ranches, our eggs local farms—well, ours actually come from our own chickens. We buy grains from either local farmers or through a bulk buying situation. Our produce is from the seasonal farmers market, our own garden, gardens of others, our buying club, or the local health food store. We also order several items online. We buy some things from major supermarkets, but those numbers are small.

Stocking your pantry for the lowest amount of money possible does take some effort, but it can be done! Depending on your own personal goals, you may be able to build a wonderfully stocked real food pantry that will save you money and time, and give you peace of mind.

Meet the Pantry

During the course of this book, I'll use the word *pantry* often. In many ways, pantry will be a generic term. When I refer to pantry, I don't just mean the nice big walk-in pantry in many homes. I also mean cabinets, cupboards, baker's racks, shelving, or any other place you keep your food items. Pantry, used generically, also refers to your freezer, either as part of your refrigerator or separate. Pantry could also refer to a cellar, or a room in your basement functioning as a cellar. It could refer to a dedicated section of your garage, shed, or attic. Pantry can even mean underneath the bed, in the coat closet, under the couch, behind the books on the bookshelf, any miscellaneous drawer where you've stashed food, or even in a hope chest. I hope you get the idea that *pantry* basically refers to any place you've chosen to store food.

I think it's important to note that, while I mention the garage, shed, or attic, these may or may not be good places to keep food. Depending on your physical location and your weather, these places may be too hot or too cold for year-round food storage. According to the California Department of Education, fifty degrees is the recommended temperature for dry goods to have the maximum shelf life. However, seventy degrees is adequate for dry storage of most products. Keeping that in mind, a range of fifty to seventy degrees Fahrenheit is probably a good rule of thumb.

Depending on your goals for stocking your pantry, you may need to get creative in your own pantry solutions. Whether you live in a studio apartment or palatial spread, you *can* have a well-stocked pantry.

Building a Real Food Pantry

When thinking about the foods you want in your pantry, it's important to think about what you eat. There's a saying in food storage circles to "eat what you store and store what you eat." Whether you're stocking a pantry focused on food storage or focused on saving time and money, the principle remains. I promise, if you're stocking up on things your family won't eat, you won't save anything.

When we first began our transition from a Standard American Diet to a real, whole, traditional foods diet (from this point on, simply referred to as a real food diet), we had a few challenges figuring out how to stock our pantry. We've been continuing to figure out what works for us combined with how we normally eat.

Eating real food and having a well-stocked pantry *is* possible.

One of the things with real food is real food spoils. Finding items with a long shelf life that still meet the real food criteria is important, and it's what we aim for with *most* of our pantry additions.

Affording the products needed to fill up the pantry is another concern. Because we choose to buy many items that are higher quality and usually on the expensive side, our food budget gets a bit of a stretching anyway. Is it possible to add the purchasing of bulk items into a food budget without increasing the budgeted amount? Yes! It can be done. It may take longer to reach your goals, but it will be worth it.

For our real foods diet, we aim to follow the Dietary Guidelines established by the Weston A. Price Foundation. We focus our food dollars on naturally raised meats, fresh milk from animals on pasture, farm-fresh eggs from free-range chickens, and traditional fats. We eat fresh fruits and vegetables—organic as often as possible. We use whole grains, nuts, seeds, and legumes that have been properly prepared to help eliminate the phytic acid and other anti-nutrients. And we throw in a good dose of fermented and cultured foods to help improve the health of our guts. My hope is that, in this handbook, you'll see how following a diet based on real foods can meld wonderfully with a well-stocked pantry.

Before You Begin

To get the most bang for your buck and to help with staying organized, having a plan is a great place to begin.

In order to formulate your plan to stock your own real food pantry, you might want to start with asking yourself a few questions.

A good first question is, why do I want to stock my pantry?

Do you want to have a few things on hand in case you can't make it to the market? Are you following the recommendations of FEMA to keep a three-day supply of nonperishable foods on hand in case you're hit by an unexpected storm? Would you like to build your pantry up in order to save money and shop the pantry first? Are you looking to take your pantry up a notch and store a year or more of food to prepare for any unexpected emergencies (job loss, natural disaster, etc.)?

Knowing your end goal will help when you're formulating your plan to stock your pantry.

Once you know why you're stocking your pantry, you'll want to zero in on just how much you wish to stock.

If your goal for your pantry is to make sure you have a few days' worth of food on hand, just in case you can't get to the store, then you won't need to spend too much time planning or shopping to fill your pantry.

If your goal is to have a seven-year supply of food, reminiscent of Joseph in the Bible, then you'll need to have a well thought out plan and spend some time accumulating everything. You'd probably also want to have some sort of inventory system (spreadsheets, a computer program, or even just a big notebook) and may even need to find or build a separate storage area.

Chances are good you're going to want to have enough food in your pantry to accommodate somewhere between those few days and seven years. You don't have to know exactly how much to begin stocking your pantry, but a general idea will help in the long run and might even save you time and money.

When we first became serious about stocking our pantry, we had a goal of three months' worth of shelf-stable food plus a seasonally full freezer. We stock our freezer each fall during hunting season and don't worry about it again until the next fall, with the exception of a monthly beef CSA (Community Supported Agriculture) Share.

In 2012, we chose to work on a year of shelf-stable storage. As I'm writing this, we're still working toward this goal. We estimate we have around nine months of shelf-stable food, which is a decent amount to have on hand and an amount that stores well in our somewhat small house.

To plan for one year of food, I set up a couple of spreadsheets to keep track while we were making our purchases. Once we reached our "happy point," our inventory method became quite simple.

Calculating

Figuring out how much food a family needs for twelve months can get interesting. There are several popular ways to come up with these amounts. Here are four ways I've either used or considered.

The first and possibly simplest way, which requires the least amount of planning, is the Fab Four or Big Four. With this method, you'd store wheat, salt, honey and powdered milk: four hundred pounds of wheat, twenty pounds of salt, ten pounds of honey, and sixty pounds of powdered milk per person. This is very simple, needs very little planning, and is fairly economical. Just do the math and buy the amounts.

However, this plan has some serious issues. And even though I'm mentioning it, we immediately knew this plan wouldn't work for us. Powdered milk isn't something we're comfortable consuming. It's extremely high in oxidized cholesterol due to the processing. Oxidized cholesterol is believed to contribute to heart disease and cancer. The second problem with this method is the high amount of wheat. While we aren't wheat-free, I have a hard time believing that a diet composed mainly of wheat could be healthy. I *believe* eating that much wheat could lead to wheat sensitivity. The third problem is the lack of variety. While these ingredients could create several different meals, sooner or later, eating the same thing every day is going to be a problem.

The second way, which I sort of used when figuring out our three-month pantry, is to make a menu plan for the week, write down every ingredient and quantity needed for each dish, and buy that amount. You'd then have a one-week supply of food. Repeat for as many weeks as needed. I found this to work well to a point and did use this to loosely come up with three months of food. I feel this method gave us a very good start.

The third way to calculate food storage amounts is to use a calorie per day system. How many calories do you need per day? How many people are in your family? How many days of food storage do you want? This could work very well if you're storing foods that have the calorie count on them. If you're cooking foods from scratch, such as beans, grains, and meats, then you'll need to do a little more math. How many calories are in a pound of beans? In a pound of grain? In a pound of meat?

And finally, the fourth way for calculating food storage is pounds per person. In the resources, I list a link to a simple calculator put out by the LDS church. I've heard from several sources that this calculator figures the bare minimum amounts for survival. And if you take a look at the calculator, you'll notice many of the foods listed aren't exactly real food friendly, and there isn't any meat or produce listed with this calculator.

I'm sure that there are other methods for calculating twelve months of food storage that I haven't mentioned.

What we decided to do was to use the food storage calculator as a guide and substitute foods we don't eat with foods we do eat.

I put together a spreadsheet showing the calculator suggestions on one side and our choices on the other side. I figured, as long as I ended up with somewhere near the same quantities in each category, it'd work out well. After chatting with a friend, who also does food storage, and learning that she's storing a large amount of seeds and nuts, we adjusted our spreadsheet to add in more of those, not only because of the excellent nutrition nuts and seeds provide, but also because they don't need to be cooked. Instant food! One final note on the spreadsheet, everything on it are foods we already eat and like. We didn't want to buy a bunch of stuff we had never tried before!

What's Next?

Once the spreadsheet is figured, it's filled in with quantities based on family size. Also, if you're planning on an amount of more than a few months, you'll need to gather supplies for long-term storage. You'll need buckets with lids, mylar bags, and oxygen absorbers.

We found bakeries to be an economical source for buckets, but it's a slow process since they don't always have them. In our town, the bucket price varies depending on who's working in the bakery. One time, I got five buckets with lids for a dollar. Usually the buckets are a dollar each, and the lids are fifty cents each. These buckets have been filled with frosting, so they did need to be cleaned out. We like to have both five-gallon buckets and three-gallon buckets. The three-gallons are perfect for storing most twenty-five-pound bags. Some of our purchases were in fifty-pound quantities, for which we use a five-gallon bucket and a second partial bucket. Three 50-pound bags are just about perfect for four 5-gallon buckets. We also have several one-gallon buckets for overflow and smaller quantities of items.

I ordered mylar bags from Amazon, but there are other sources available on the internet. We ordered five-gallon bags plus oxygen absorbers and one-gallon bags plus oxygen absorbers. I have to admit, the first time we used the bags and oxygen absorbers was a little stressful. I was so worried about doing it wrong! But it worked out fine, and everything sealed well. You can find many YouTube videos showing people sealing up buckets of food.

We used the iron (is it bad that the main use my iron has seen in several years is sealing mylar bags?) and a 2" x 2" board that Joe had left over from a building project. Keep in mind, the oxygen absorbers do just that—absorb oxygen. Once the sealed bag they come in is open, they begin absorbing. They actually get hot. We put ours in a jar and only opened the jar as needed, making sure to use up the jar in the same day.

Another item we found helpful for packaging our food storage was a vacuum sealer. I like the rolls that can be cut into any size bag. These work really well for storing home dehydrated foods, nuts, seeds, and similar items.

Where Are You Going to Put It All?

One reason we originally stopped at a three-month pantry was because of space. We lived in a double-wide mobile home and didn't have much of a pantry or closet space. We didn't have any extra rooms, no basement, and no root cellar. We did have a 10' x 10' storage shed and a slightly over sized two-car, freestanding garage. I was already using the cold end of our bedroom closet for ferments, olive oil, and other things that store well in a cold space, plus a few five-gallon buckets. The kitchen and dining room were well utilized. Under beds were used for storage (much to my sixteen-year-old's dismay), as well as bookshelves.

Joe and I started looking around the house at various areas to put things. It's amazing the space you can find once you really start to look. One thing that helped with our space was purchasing large metal storage shelves that we could adjust to fit our buckets. We covered a wall with these and then put curtains over the shelves. This really increased our ability to store things, and it looks pretty good.

When first thinking about food storage, it's tempting to think, "Okay, this month we'll buy all of our grains and next month all of our beans." While this seems like a good idea, it could backfire. What if next month the car breaks down and you can't buy the beans? And then the dreaded layoff occurs? You've got a whole lot of grains to eat but nothing to go with them.

Spreading out your purchases among each category or using the weekly menu plan method ensures that you'll have a variety.

Water

When you start thinking about your pantry, I believe the very, very first thing you should do before you begin any thoughts of food is to think about water. Whether you're planning to stock your pantry for just a few days or for several years, water is something that should be a focus.

You might think you don't need to worry about water since you can turn on the tap and there it is. You may remember from my own "big storm" story that the town near us had their water knocked out for several days. And if you happen to be on a well instead of city water, your pump will probably not work without power, which means no water coming out of the tap.

FEMA recommends storing one gallon of water per person, per day for three days. That's a great start with your water storage. Water is an incredibly important item for your pantry. You cannot live without water for longer than three days.

Keep in mind, besides for drinking, you'll need water for cooking, hygiene, and cleaning. Water is important. There are lots of containers on the market for storing water, in all sorts of price ranges. Most of our water storage is in two-liter soda bottles that kept appearing around here when my older children lived with us. I do have a few bottles of store-bought water (the gallon size and also individual water bottles), but we rotate those regularly. I worry the plastic in the gallon containers will break down since it's so thin.

Another thing to think about, what if the event that knocked out your water lasts longer than your water storage? Three days of water storage wasn't enough for many of the people that have been affected by major hurricanes, tornadoes, and other storms in recent years. Are you in a disaster-prone area? If so, it might make sense to store more than three days of water. Or is there a river, lake, or creek nearby that you can get water from?

If you plan to use a water source like that to get additional water, you'll need a way to purify it. We have a Berkey Water Filter System that we use for all our drinking water, which is suitable for filtering water from other sources, including rainwater. You could also plan on boiling all your water or purifying it in another manner. An internet search should give you many ideas on how to accomplish these things.

Heat and Eat

Our experience of being without power for those few days really made us realize just how important it is to have food available that takes very little effort to prepare. The house we lived in when the power went out was entirely electric. Without power, the stove and oven didn't work—neither did the heat, but that's a subject for another time.

We did have a camp stove that we used for preparing our meals. Since we had several boxed and canned items on hand (remember, we were on a Standard American Diet at that time), it took very little effort to heat those meals up on the stove.

Fast forward to now. On a real food diet, most of our food takes some time and effort to prepare. While food preparation doesn't take a ton of time, it isn't as easy as opening a can and heating it up. A good portion of our food requires extended cooking times. Because we wanted to have some foods on hand that could be put together quickly in case of an emergency, we created a Heat and Eat Bin.

Heat and Eat Bin

I think it's important to remember that canned food, overall, has less nutrition than fresh food. Many real food enthusiasts choose to never eat food from a can. If that's you, then you probably don't want to create a Heat and Eat Bin.

For us, this truly is a bin. I have one of those large Rubbermaid-style containers that became designated as the Heat and Eat Bin.

In this bin are foods that require no preparation other than opening up the can or jar and (sometimes) heating up the contents. They're convenience-style foods, not the foods we eat every day. One reason for them to live in the bin is to keep them out of the everyday foods.

While these are convenience foods, they're items I purchase after scouring the ingredients lists and deciding they're okay for the intended purposes. The intended purpose is for emergency use.

That emergency may be a power outage. However, depending on the duration of the outage, the bin may or may not come into play. Our outage in the Pacific Northwest lasted from Sunday until Friday. Using that scenario, we would first eat any food in our fridge before busting into the Heat and Eat Bin. If there was an event that left the possibility of a longer-term power outage, then the heat-and-eat foods would be welcome during that time of transition. If a large regional event happened to knock the power out long term, not having to think about meals for a couple of days could be helpful.

Another great thing about having the bin is that it's portable. If we're ever in a situation where we need to leave home in a hurry, we can grab our Heat and Eat Bin and our camping bin, which happen to be conveniently located right next to each other. These can be a great addition to a 72-hour bag.

Not sure what a 72-hour bag is? A 72-hour bag is a collection of basic items your family may need in the event of an emergency. FEMA recommends having a kit of your own food, water, and other supplies to last seventy-two hours in case you need to survive on your own after an emergency. This kit, often referred to as a Bug-Out Bag or BOB, should be portable in case you need to evacuate.

The Heat and Eat Bin can also be quite convenient for times when I'm under the weather and someone else is cooking. One thing we've noticed is, while the foods are okay, they're certainly not as tasty as foods we prepare ourselves. Originally, I thought the children might be tempted to open a can of soup as a snack (that's part of the reason for stashing them in a bin), but after eating a can recently, my youngest daughter declared it didn't taste as good as she expected. She didn't go as far as to say my cooking was better, but it was still nice to hear.

I go through the bin every six months or so to make sure everything in the bin is still fresh. I check expiration dates, and if anything is getting close, I remove it from the bin and we use it up. While these expiration dates aren't the date the product is no longer safe to use, it just makes sense to us to keep things current. New supplies are purchased or prepared for the bin as soon as possible.

What Kind of Things Are in the Bin?

FEMA recommends a three-day supply of food for emergency kits, so that's where we started with our Heat and Eat Bin.

What worked for me was to make a three-day menu plan and use that as a guide for stocking our bin.

Also in the bin are miscellaneous items, like a can opener, disposable dishes and silverware, salt, pepper, a roll of toilet paper, and a jug of water. These things are there specifically in case of needing to take the bin and go. Our camping bin does have some of the same items in it also, but if it were to be left behind and we didn't have a can opener, it might be challenging to get our cans open!

Do You Need a Heat and Eat Bin As Part of Your Food Storage?

Maybe or maybe not.

You may choose to keep your three-day emergency food only in your BOB or just in your cabinets. But it's smart to have three days of emergency food somewhere. If you aren't comfortable with canned foods, you'll need to find an alternative. Jerky and/or pemmican plus other dehydrated items might work for you.

Beans & Legumes

After you have your water storage and three days of quick to prepare foods, the next place to focus your efforts might be beans and legumes.

Why Beans?

Beans are usually reasonably priced, even when buying organic; have a wonderful shelf life; and can be prepared in a variety of tasty ways. Beans also have a wonderful nutritional profile containing magnesium, potassium, phosphorus, folate, and many other important nutrients.

Plus, when you add inexpensive beans to your menu plans, you can free up additional food dollars to put toward stocking your pantry or toward other high-quality food items.

Early on, when my family was transitioning from a Standard American Diet to a real food diet, we didn't have the ability to increase our food budget. By eating beans several times per week, we were able to afford small quantities of more expensive items, like grass-fed beef and a cow share for real milk.

I've purchased beans and legumes for as little as forty-two cents a pound in twenty-five-pound bags. If you purchase these in your local grocers off the shelf, you'll likely pay more than that, but they're still very reasonable. Depending on your own pantry goals, you could choose to buy beans in one-pound quantities, or in twenty-five or even fifty-pound bags like we do. Pick a variety or two of beans you enjoy. These could be pinto beans, garbanzo beans, lima beans, lentils, white beans, black beans, red beans, or any kind of bean you want. These beans come dry and have a decent shelf life.

Where to Purchase?

Check locally first! Depending on your location, there could be farmers in your area growing crops of beans and legumes. This is often the least expensive and highest quality source for these. Be sure to ask questions of your farmer. Is the farmer organic certified? If not, does he or she follow organic practices? We were very happy to get two bags of beans from a farm in Wyoming recently. These beans seem much fresher than any other beans we've used, and they cook up wonderfully. They also taste terrific. Finding these beans has inspired us to research growing beans in our own garden. The freshness is absolutely amazing.

One of my main resources for beans is Azure Standard. This company offers once a month delivery service of sorts by taking orders to a "drop point." You can go to the Azure Standard website (azurestandard.com) for more information on drops that may be in your area. For the most part, we've been happy with the beans from Azure, but the farmer beans cook considerably quicker, which leads me to believe they're fresher than the Azure beans.

You may also have a buying club or co-op in your area to purchase these bulk products. Amazon is also a very popular source for bulk products, but do pay attention to shipping costs. I've noticed sometimes the shipping exceeds the product.

Another option that I've heard people have success with is to go to your local (private or chain) grocery store or health food store and ask the manager to order bulk items for you. This option might work very well for saving on shipping costs. Some chain stores also have websites where you can order directly from them; they'll even waive the shipping costs once you reach a price threshold.

Preparing Beans

Beans and legumes—like grains, nuts, and seeds—need to be soaked prior to cooking. By soaking, you'll help to make the beans more digestible. I'm sure we're all familiar with the reputation that beans carry!

Even with soaking, some people will still have difficulty digesting beans and will suffer the side effects. KerryAnn from Cooking Traditional Foods remedies that in her house by sprouting all her beans before cooking them. Definitely something to try if this is an issue for you or someone you love.

Back to soaking, some beans need to be soaked, not only in plain water, but in water with an acidic medium added. I refer to the list put out by the Weston A. Price Foundation in the article "Putting the Polish on Those Humble Beans". But I have to admit, sometimes I totally forget to check my list and soak my beans in just plain water or throw in some apple cider vinegar or whey "just in case" it's needed for that type of bean. Oops. You should probably be more exact than I am.

Once the beans have soaked for anywhere from ten to twenty-four hours, depending on the type of bean (and maybe how your day has gone), the soaking water needs to be drained off. Then you have a choice to make.

To Sprout or Not to Sprout?

I've already mentioned KerryAnn sprouts all of her beans prior to cooking to help with digestion. At this point, that isn't what I do, but I do sprout *some* beans and legumes depending on what my final intentions are for those beans.

I really like to sprout lentils and whole peas. I often sprout garbanzo beans. Occasionally, I'll sprout other beans.

I sprout my beans in a colander. It's super easy to sprout in this manner. I use the colander that the beans were drained in when removing the soaking water. I rinse the beans and then cover them with a dish towel, leaving them in the sink for the time being to drain. When I need to use my sink, I simply put a plate on the counter and move the colander/towel contraption to the plate. The beans need to be rinsed at least twice daily.

When are the sprouts finished? That's a great question! They're finished when you decide they're finished. Sprout People is a great resource for all things "sprout." They recommend keeping short tails (1/16 to 1/4 inch), but more importantly, tasting the bean or legume each time you rinse your sprouts until they taste good to you. I usually let my sprouts go for a couple of days. You may sprout for a longer or shorter amount of time, depending on your personal preferences.

Cooking Without Sprouting

I grew up eating beans. My mama would make a large pot of pinto beans almost every Friday night. Quite often I had the task of helping to cook the beans. This meant I had to stir them so they didn't burn. I hate to admit that I scorched the beans on more than one occasion. I remember being very happy one time when I found an article in a magazine that stated, if the beans are scorched on the bottom, to carefully remove the top layers of beans without disturbing the burnt-on part. I happily told my mama about this. She wisely responded, *"Don't burn the beans in the first place."* Hmmm. Sounds pretty smart.

My usual method in my own kitchen to avoid burning the beans in the first place is to use my crockpot. I put my drained beans in the crockpot and cover them with liquid—either water or broth—plug the pot in, turn it on low, and walk away. Around eight hours later, the beans are ready to season and eat. So easy! An Instant Pot, or other type of pressure cooker, is also a wonderful way to cook beans—and very quick!

Cooking Sprouted Beans

After the beans have been sprouted, you may still wish to cook them, depending on what you plan to do with those beans and your own personal preferences. We prefer the taste of steamed lentils or peas as opposed to raw. If you do this, taste the steaming legumes every five to ten minutes until they taste the way you want.

If I sprout larger beans, I may cook those in water on the stove top (remembering my mama's advice) for forty-five minutes to an hour until they're soft. Sprouted beans cook very quickly, and you should check them often to avoid them turning to mush. I'm at a high altitude, so your beans may cook much quicker.

Bean Recipes

A quick search of the internet will yield many bean recipes. I'll share a few links to get you started.

On my website I share our 13-week rotating menu, which features a pot of beans each week turned into three or four different dishes. This is a concept known as Stretchy Beans that I learned about several years ago on a blog that no longer exists (appropriately named Lentils and Rice). I'm sure you'll find a bean recipe (or ten) that you love during those thirteen weeks.

Wardee from GNOWFGLINS has a great bean page that includes information on soaking, cooking, and dry bean yield, plus links to some of her recipes. This is a wonderful resource.

A very popular eBook is *The Everything Beans Book* by Katie Kimball of Kitchen Stewardship. I put off buying her book for some time because I was already the "bean guru and knew everything there was to know about beans" (read with tongue in cheek). After hearing so many great things, I realized I might be missing out on something (and I never want to miss out on things), so I went ahead and ordered the book. All the reports were correct! This is a terrific eBook with tons of wonderful information and recipes. I may just have to relinquish my title of bean guru to Katie Kimball!

Use Those Beans

Now that you have some direction to preparing your beans, start using them! While beans do have a long shelf life, as they age, they dry out even more and need a longer time to cook. I found some old beans in my pantry once, and I think I cooked those about twelve hours and they were still rock hard! Keep in mind, when you purchase beans, they may already be several months old, especially if you're buying them off the grocery store shelf. You can seal beans in mylar bags or in a vacuum sealer to help extend their shelf life.

Also, use those beans as part of your overall pantry stocking plan. I've already mentioned how, when we first started real food, beans were a regular on our menu so that we could afford higher-quality ingredients to use sparingly. When we got serious about stocking our real food pantry, we once again focused on beans.

During the winter of 2010–2011, we ate beans three or four times each week. The money we saved by eating beans went toward bulk buys (more beans!) to help us reach our pantry stocking goals. While your family may not wish to or need to eat beans as often as we did, keep in mind that it's a possibility. Properly prepared beans (soaked and/or sprouted) can be a wonderful addition to a real food diet. Combined with small amounts of meat and liberal amounts of broth, you'll still be getting terrific nutrition.

Concentrate on Fats

In my opinion, fats are the most important item in my pantry. Fats have developed a bad rap over the years, but this wasn't always the case.

I love reading historical fiction books—books set during the time of the settlers or pioneers. I read these books before we began our real food journey and remember reading one where the heroines were talking about how badly they wished for duck fat to make biscuits. I have to admit, I didn't do much cooking during that time, so I didn't realize how important fat was for biscuits, but I did think, "Wow, don't they know about the dangers of fat?" Oops. Turns out they were right; I was wrong.

Why are fats important in your pantry? Fats are essential for your health. They help with brain function, enhance the immune system, help with leaky gut, and help you feel full longer, along with a whole other host of benefits. <u>You need fats in your diet.</u> Not to mention, they help you prepare foods. Think about the meals you make; now think how difficult it'd be without any fat or oil.

Very Important!

You don't want to store rancid, fake fats. Grocery store shortening, canola, vegetable oil and the like are FAKE fats that will harm you instead of helping you. Pay particular attention if it says "heart healthy" on the package, because if it says that, it's probably not.

I'd recommend reading up on fats and what we've been led to believe about them. "The Oiling of America," from the Weston A. Price Foundation, is a great article that details the trouble with fake fats.

You need traditional fats in your diet. Our pantry contains coconut oil, olive oil, palm oil, and animal fats. We're still light on animal fats since we only get those when processing our poultry, but I guess you could say we store those on the foot.

Where to Purchase?

Fats are my most expensive pantry item. I've found that ordering in bulk (a five-gallon bucket for my family of five) is the cheapest way to purchase coconut oil, but it's still a chunk of change to put out at one time. Five gallons last my family around a year, and the price per gallon is substantially less in this size than buying just one gallon at a time. Sales or free shipping really help with the cost. I order olive oil and palm oil by the gallon—again, I use sales or free shipping. I've also started storing ghee. I love ghee for cooking, and it has an excellent shelf life. When I find a great deal on butter, I stash a few extra pounds in the freezer. We'll talk more later specifically about freezer storage.

For other animal fats, you can contact local farmers or ranchers and ask about getting fat to render yourself to tallow or lard. I spoke to a farmer I know about this, and he said he'd let me know next time he has it available. Making friends with farmers and ranchers can be very beneficial to helping you stock your pantry for less!

Grains and Grain Alternatives

Grains are a terrific thing to add to your pantry—provided, of course, that your family eats grains. We like to keep a variety of grains and flours in our pantry.

It wasn't too long ago when the only "grains" we stored were white flour and white rice. Now, I'm pretty sure white flour doesn't even qualify as anything more than an ingredient for making papier Mache. Instead, we store wheat berries. Wheat berries are the actual grains of wheat, ready to be ground up to make into whole wheat flour, or cooked to use as cereal, or even sprouted to use in salads or other ways. They're a wonderful and very adaptable ingredient to my real food kitchen.

Wheat berries are available in assorted varieties, and each behaves slightly different when baking. I like to keep both hard red and hard white wheat berries, plus soft white wheat berries on hand. The soft white berries make wonderful pastry flour for cakes and cookies. The hard white sprouts beautifully for salads and also makes nice "white" bread. And the hard red is our "everyday" wheat made into sourdough loaves and is especially wonderful for making a hearty artisan loaf.

Rye berries are also a family favorite. I keep them on hand mainly for turning into rye flour for my sourdough starter. I find that rye flour makes a wonderfully light and active sourdough starter. I combine the rye-based starter with any kind of wheat, depending on what I wish my final product to be. Sourdough cake is made with the rye starter and soft white wheat for a delicious treat. Artisan bread or our everyday sourdough is made with hard red wheat. Of course, these aren't really "rules" that I follow, rather guidelines open to experimentation.

In addition to wheat berries, we also keep other things that can be ground into flour. Spelt is a "cousin" to wheat and is another great item for grinding into flour. Many people enjoy eating and working with spelt more than wheat, and even though it does contain gluten, some people find they can eat spelt in place of wheat. We don't have any specific food intolerances, so we just enjoy spelt for what it is: an alternative to wheat. Spelt is more expensive than wheat, so we store less of it. Working with spelt is slightly different than working with wheat. I recommend reading up and experimenting with it before stocking an excessive amount of spelt.

Another item I really enjoy is kamut. This is another form of wheat with a buttery and nutty flavor. It's especially wonderful when turned into pasta. The whole berries also make a nice cold salad, lending a chewy and flavor-packed texture.

We keep several other grains on hand, not usually for turning into flour, but for leaving whole to cook or sprout as a side dish or salad. Millet, quinoa, and brown rice are terrific for this. And remember that white rice I mentioned in the first paragraph? We do still store white rice. I know many real food enthusiasts aren't okay with white rice. We are for a couple of reasons. First, it stores very well. Brown rice doesn't store as well, and if long-term storage is the goal, white rice is suitable. The second reason, we like white rice. In our everyday life, we tend to alternate between brown rice and white rice. This is a great compromise for us.

Keep in mind when storing whole grains that if you wish to turn these grains into flour, you'll need a flour mill or grinder. We have an electric mill that works great and produces flour in almost no time. We also have a hand-crank grinder to use in case we're ever without power and need to grind flour. Until recently, our crank grinder was not very high grade. Whenever we used it, I was reminded of the Laura Ingalls Wilder book *The Long Winter* and how someone had to be grinding wheat continuously in order to have enough flour for gruel. We were recently able to upgrade to a higher-quality grinder that's much easier to use. However, it's still a manual grinder, and manual does mean work!

In addition to grains, we also store grain alternatives. We have coconut flour and almond flour, plus other nuts that can be turned into nut flours. If you're grain free, you'd want to concentrate on these items. I like having these items on hand for making quick baked goods. Sourdough bread takes all day to make, but coconut flour bread takes only a few minutes to mix up and then time to bake. This comes in handy on the days I don't plan properly.

Where to Purchase

Once again, check with your local farmer first. Depending on your area, grains might be an item you can find locally. Be sure to ask about organic practices, if that's a concern. Another thing to think about is GMO (Genetically Modified Organism). Until recently, I felt confident that wheat was a "safe" item. While wheat has been hybridized and changed over the years (no doubt, the wheat available to us now isn't the wheat of the Bible), it was not a commercial GMO crop. However, a field of GMO wheat was recently found in Oregon. Could this mean that the commercial wheat crop has now been GMO contaminated? No one knows for sure.

We get wheat from Azure Standard. They have an excellent selection of organic wheat for a reasonable price. We buy in twenty-five- or fifty-pound bags. We buy whole wheat and grind it ourselves, but Azure also has ground wheat (flour), which is what I purchased before investing in a mill. If you purchase flour, the shelf life is drastically reduced. You won't want to purchase more than you can use within a few months' time. Wheat berries, on the other hand, will keep for years when properly stored—some sources say thirty years.

When we get our wheat and grains, we stick them in the freezer for seventy-two hours to "kill" anything that came along. This is an important step. One time, I ordered five pounds of brown rice and stuck it in a glass jar. When I went to use the rice a few months later, I noticed the rice was moving. *Yuck!* There were bugs in my rice. Apparently, this is very common, but it totally grossed me out. Luckily, that was the only rice affected, but it taught me a good lesson to freeze the grains to kill anything.

After the freezer time, we put our wheat in long-term storage by using mylar bags with oxygen absorbers inside a three- or five-gallon bucket. There are many sources on the internet for these packaging materials. I usually order ours from Amazon. We get our buckets from the bakeries in town, but you can also order buckets on the internet or purchase them in big box hardware stores. Be sure to look for food-quality buckets.

We've also found that some of our grains work better in small packages—either one-gallon mylar bags with oxygen absorbers or packaged using a vacuum sealer—that way we only need to open and use up a small amount at a time instead of a large bag. We use the smaller bags for things like quinoa and nut flours.

If you aren't stocking your pantry for long-term storage, your grains will probably be fine in glass jars or similar containers on a shelf.

Seasonings and Spices

I absolutely love having a large selection of seasonings and spices on hand. By keeping a variety of different spices, I can easily change the flavors of our meals and create new dishes. By taking a large pot of beans and dividing it into three dishes, each spiced differently, we can feel like we're eating something new and special each night instead of the "same old beans."

We started our seasoning stock with the basics: sea salt and pepper. We added in other things like cumin, chili powder, powdered garlic, curry powder, cinnamon, nutmeg, etc. as our budget permitted.

Where to Purchase

We don't buy those little jars of spices in the grocery store. Not only are they overpriced, they're also almost always irradiated. The process of irradiation uses ionized radiation to increase shelf life and kill bacteria. This leaves a "dead" product with zero medicinal qualities and *could* cause cancer.

We buy most of our spices through Azure Standard due to the fact that they aren't irradiated, and also the bulk pricing is quite good. We've found some very good spices in our local health food store. I've also heard good things about some online sources for spices, herbs, and seasonings, but I haven't used any of these.

I do recommend, if you're unsure of the flavor of a certain spice or seasoning, try a small quantity first before buying it by the pound. Believe me when I tell you, purchasing a pound of a spice you only like so-so is not cost effective. It will likely go stale before you can use it.

Preserved Foods

Canned goods and real food don't really go hand in hand. When eating a real food diet, we want to eat food that will spoil; canned goods don't fit that bill. At our house, we do use some canned goods, either from a commercial source or home canned, for ease of meal preparation and our longer-term storage. But before we talk about actual canned goods, I want to briefly discuss my first two choices for food preservation: lacto-fermentation and dehydration.

Lacto-Fermented Items

This is a very important element to my pantry. Fermenting is a wonderful way to extend the life of vegetables, fruits, and even meats. Not to mention the nutritional benefits of fermenting. Fermenting can make the food more digestible (especially vegetables) plus increase vitamins, produce enzymes, and even add to our overall gut health. You want a healthy gut! Ferments can help make that happen. And if you're in times of stress, maintaining a healthy gut is going to be essential.

The only drawback with keeping fermented items in your pantry is the fact that they need to be kept in cold storage. A refrigerator works perfect for this, but if you're like me, you have limited space in your fridge. You might consider a second fridge (try freecycle.org to find a free one); or if you have a cellar, that will work wonderfully for cold storage. We don't have a second fridge or a cellar (we have plans to put in a cellar in the near future), but I do have a very cold closet. My ferments store just fine in this space. Depending on your location (I'm in Wyoming, it gets cold here), you might have a similar place to keep your ferments. Or you may be able to come up with some other makeshift cold storage space.

Dehydrated Items

I'm totally enthralled with dehydrating! Being able to take vegetables, fruits, and even meats and turn them into a shelf-stable item that weighs practically nothing and takes up very little room is spectacular. My dehydrator is just a little, round, thirty or forty dollar thing, but it works just fine. In the future, I do hope to have a larger dehydrator so I can do more items at one time. You might be surprised to discover all the different types of things that can be dehydrated—I know I was. I love the Backpacking Chef website for great ideas and suggestions on things to dehydrate. One of the great things about doing your own dehydrating is you can choose the raw ingredients that you're starting with. You know that you're using organic or pastured items. I'm currently taking the Dehydrating eCourse by GNOWFGLINS.

Home Canned

Home canning is something that I'm learning, thanks to lessons from friends. I've done water bath canning a few times and have had lessons in pressure canning. I have all the equipment needed for both but haven't taken the time to really pursue it. I believe there's a place for home canning in a real food kitchen. Yes, you'll lose some of the nutrients in canning, but if you compare your home preserved goods to the commercial counterpart, the choice is clear: home preserved. You know exactly what went into that jar; you know the quality of the ingredients you started with.

While my home preservation experience is still new, I do have goals. A friend gave me a lesson in canning meats, and they turned out great! We live in Wyoming where hunting opportunities are abundant. By having the option to can some of the meat, we can really increase our wild game supply. Our home-grown chickens would also be good for canning. Right now, I can't quite fit enough chicken in the freezer to last until the next year (too much antelope and deer in there!) If I can combine the freezer with canning, that'd be wonderful. Plus, I hear canned chicken is quite tasty, especially in chicken salad sandwiches. Beans are another item I want to can. I love the idea of having jars of properly soaked beans that I can just open up and have ready in an instant. Broth is also on my list for the same reason. I intend to can fruit and some vegetables. Most of my vegetables I plan to ferment as space allows. Obviously, the biggest advantage to canning over fermenting is the lack of a need for cold storage. Canned food is shelf stable.

Setting up for home canning does have some expense involved. I have a water bath canner and a pressure canner. The pressure canner is a must for canning meats, beans, and broth. And when canning, new lids are required with each batch.

Commercially Canned

Finally, let's discuss commercially canned items. Yes, I do believe there's a place for commercially canned items in a real food kitchen and food storage. Label reading is super important when choosing these items. Some commercially canned goods I use are salmon, tuna, coconut milk, tomatoes, tomato paste, pimentos, olives, and artichoke hearts. Okay, some of these items I buy in jars, but in my mind, they still count as canned.

I understand that not everyone feels it's okay to use any canned goods in a real food pantry. If you aren't okay with canned items, don't stock them in your pantry. Personally, I'm okay with the few canned goods we do use, at least as an interim item. I hope someday to be able to eliminate some of these items. Home canned and dehydrated tomatoes will replace commercially canned (if my garden ever cooperates), and we'll use less salmon and tuna and more home canned chicken. But for now, I'll continue to have these commercial products and combine them with my ferments.

Sweeteners

Sweeteners are an important group in my pantry. While we try to limit our sweet treats, keeping a good selection of unrefined sweeteners on hand makes meal and snack preparation much easier. Whole, unrefined sweeteners like honey, maple syrup, dates, and raisins come in quite handy for preparing smoothies, ice creams, and custards. Sucanat or Rapadura—dehydrated cane sugar—makes a terrific substitute for refined white or brown sugar in small amounts.

Honey is a wonderful sweetener to keep on hand. Local, raw honey isn't only a sweetener but can also help with seasonal allergies, allowing it to do double duties as a natural remedy. For maximum benefits, raw honey should be kept raw. Heating above 117 degrees will kill the beneficial enzymes in honey. We love to use honey for sweet treats like delicious raw fudge. With only coconut oil, cocoa powder, and honey, it goes together easily and makes a wonderful and almost decadent dessert. When using honey as a substitute for sugar, remember that honey is sweeter. I find I can use half as much honey as sugar and still get a very sweet result.

Maple syrup is rich in trace minerals and gives a wonderful flavor to items. Real maple syrup doesn't taste anything like "fake" maple syrup. While real maple syrup can be pricey, it's worth it! When shopping for maple syrup, Grade B has more minerals and flavor than A. Many people report that Amazon is a good choice for purchasing Grade B maple syrup. I often order my syrup from Azure Standard.

Dates and raisins are terrific sweeteners to use in snack bars, smoothies, and as a sweet snack on their own. Whirling them up in the food processor or blender seems to concentrate the sweetness. You may find that it doesn't take many dates to make a rather sweet smoothie.

Sucanat is dehydrated cane juice and is the perfect replacement for white or brown sugar to use in baking. Sucanat can be substituted using the same measurement that your recipe calls for, either white or brown sugar. You should know, because Sucanat is mostly unrefined, it does have a molasses flavor to it. It's very similar to brown sugar, but not much like white sugar. My family didn't notice the difference when we started using Sucanat. Your family might. While Sucanat can be substituted cup for cup in your recipes, we've found that decreasing the amount we use results in a better tasting final product. The longer we eat less processed foods, the more we notice how sweet things really are. If my recipe calls for one cup of sugar, I can easily use ¾ or even ½ of a cup and still have a very tasty treat that's less sweet.

Molasses is another sweetener that's nice to have on hand. Molasses is a by-product of white sugar production and contains many minerals. I've heard that a spoon of molasses each day will prevent grey hair! We love gingerbread made with molasses as the only sweetener. Delicious! When purchasing molasses, be sure that it's actual molasses and not brown-colored high fructose corn syrup. I order Blackstrap molasses from Azure Standard.

We do keep a small supply of pure cane sugar on hand. This is refined white sugar from sugar canes as opposed to sugar beets. Why avoid sugar beets? Sugar beets are almost 100 percent genetically modified. If you're trying to avoid GMOs, you'll want to avoid sugar beets. We use pure cane sugar for kombucha and also for guests who may be a little weirded out by putting the brown Sucanat sugar in their coffee.

Nuts and Seeds

Because of the excellent nutritional value and also the convenience of nuts and seeds, we keep a good amount of these items in our pantry.

Nuts and seeds are a more expensive item to purchase. Again, we used Azure Standard to buy bags of things in bulk. In our pantry, our main nut is almond since it's the most economical, with smaller amounts of cashews, peanuts, and hazelnuts. We also have sunflower seeds and dried coconut. In our one-year storage plan, we aim for about fifteen pounds of nuts and seeds per person. This gives us a nice amount to have on hand for snacks and as part of our meals.

Nuts and seeds store best in the shell. If storing them out of the shell, a freezer will help preserve them. After hunting season, we don't have the freezer space for nuts since we fill it with wild game. With our cold winter, they store well in the garage. When the warmer weather arrives, we move them to our freezer since it's not nearly as full after eating the wild game over the winter.

Dairy and Dairy Substitutes

This was a challenging category for me when we first started working on stocking our pantry after changing to a real food diet. In a Standard American Diet pantry, a normal item to stock would be shelf-stable powdered milk. But with the concerns of powdered milk being extremely high in oxidized cholesterol due to the processing—and oxidized cholesterol is believed to be a contributing factor to heart disease and cancer—we didn't want to rely on powdered milk.

We did find some low-heat-processed powdered milk that was supposed to be less affected by the processing system, but to be honest, it was nasty. Definitely not something we wanted to drink. It could be used for baking, but for the price, we didn't stock much of it and instead chose other items for baking.

Coconut milk turned out to be a good choice for our baking needs. I'm also exploring how to make our own nut milks and coconut milk from our storage of those items.

One of the main reasons for drinking milk is for the calcium. To help with this, we keep a supply of butter and cheese (raw, homemade) in the freezer and extra shelf-stable ghee. We also dehydrate our homemade yogurt to make a wonderful candy-like item that's high in calcium. My children love these. In our food storage, we keep several calcium rich foods: sardines, salmon (mash in the bones for extra calcium), plus canned and dehydrated leafy greens (spinach, turnip greens, mustard greens, etc.). The beans, nuts, and seeds we store also provide some calcium. These stored items, combined with extra fat (milk contains fat and is essential), work well for us.

Probably the best way to store dairy is "on the hoof." By having a dairy-producing animal, you can have ready access to milk. This isn't an option for everyone, due to space and living situations, but might be something to consider.

Another option for calcium is supplements. You may wish to consider stocking a multivitamin or specific calcium supplement and increase your fat consumption.

Miscellaneous

There are so many things that can be added to your pantry under the miscellaneous category. For us, miscellaneous is basically anything we need to prepare dishes that's not already covered in a previous category.

These are things like cocoa powder, chocolate chips, yeast, baking powder, baking soda, tea, and coffee. For this category, I thought about things I'd like to be able to make on a whim and what ingredients I'd need to make that item.

Can I make our favorite chocolate cake without running to the grocery store? How about a quick snack when unexpected guests show up?

I'm not going to go into great detail on the miscellaneous items. I'm sure, if you're anything like me, you can find plenty of extras to add into your pantry. I do find that these items, like all, are important to keep organized. In the past I've bought a special something that I thought would be great to have in my pantry, and I forgot about it. Now, I have a dedicated shelf where I put extra items that I don't often buy but want to make sure don't get misplaced.

Focus on the Freezer

For simplicity's sake, we've been considering our freezer as part of our pantry. In this chapter, we'll discuss the freezer specifically and some pros and cons of stocking the freezer. While this book is about stocking our pantry, it does cross into the realm of food storage. Food storage is something that people either love the idea of or truly dislike the idea of. For right now, we're going to switch from a stock-the-pantry mindset to a food-storage mindset. We'll do this in order to examine a con of stocking the freezer.

In food storage circles, many people believe that in order to have food storage it must all be shelf stable. I can understand this thinking. However, I think the freezer is an important component to food storage, as long as at least one thing is understood: if there's a catastrophic event in which we no longer have electricity, frozen food isn't going to stay frozen for too long (obvious, right?). I still believe in stocking up the freezer to keep food on hand and using the freezer to purchase items at the best prices.

Buying a half of a grass-fed beef is usually much more cost effective than buying by the individual cut. Stocking your freezer during hunting season with wild game can save a considerable amount of money. If you're going to stock your freezer, you may wish to consider having a plan to deal with the frozen food if there's a long-term power outage.

A generator can buy you several days just by running the freezer for a few hours each day. This can help with your time management by keeping things frozen while working on small amounts of thawed food at a time. Fermenting is an excellent food preservation method for produce, fish, and some meats. Fermented produce keeps quite well for many months; and for fish and meats, this could buy you several days or weeks. Also, fermenting is relatively quick and easy, plus ferments are extremely nutritious. Water bath and pressure canning are also options for preserving frozen food without electricity, as is dehydrating using solar power only. It may be beneficial to investigate these items so, if you're ever in a situation of a long-term power outage, you can preserve your frozen goods.

For short-term power outages, keep in mind that not opening the freezer door will help slow down the thawing process. If you have a chest freezer, you can cover it with blankets or quilts to help slow the thaw. And a full freezer stays frozen better and longer than an empty freezer. Many people fill the space in their freezer with jugs or containers of water. Okay, now that we've covered that con of freezer storage, we'll resume our talk of simply stocking the pantry.

Organization

Do you find your freezer to be a black hole? I know I do! When we only had the side-by-side freezer, I was very good about keeping inventory of what was in there. But with the addition of the chest freezer, that went by the wayside. By the end of July, we try to have both freezers as empty as possible to prepare for hunting season and chicken processing. I start the task of emptying out the freezers in June.

When I empty out the freezers, I make a list of what's left. I try to move as much food as possible to the side-by-side. Things stay much more organized on the shelves than in the "pit" of the chest freezer.

Filling the Freezer

Our freezers mainly hold wild game and home-raised chickens and ducks. They sometimes hold vegetables or fruits that have been purchased in bulk—often from Azure Standard or sometimes the farmers market—and frozen for smoothies or later use. I also like to freeze tomatoes to make lacto-fermented salsa with later in the year. My family eats salsa like candy, and it's always a nice treat to have salsa from fresh (previously frozen) tomatoes in the dead of winter.

As you choose your whole food items to put in the freezer, keep in mind that you should only store as much as you can use before the food deteriorates. Frozen food doesn't last forever. Properly packaging the foods before putting them in the freezer is also important.

A Second Freezer?

You may only need to use the freezer that's attached to the refrigerator for your frozen storage. Or you may wish to add a second freezer in the form of a chest or upright standalone freezer. While purchasing a second freezer is an investment, it may end up costing less in the long run if you're able to take advantage of discounted or bulk purchases. Do what's best for your family.

Preparing Food

Now that we've discussed a disadvantage of the freezer if the power goes out, let's consider preparing food without power. When we experienced our multiday power outage, our cook stove was entirely electric. When the power went out, we needed another option for heating food. We were fortunate that we camped fairly often and had both a small camp stove and a camp trailer with a propane stove and oven.

If the power went out at your place, would you be able to safely cook food?

If you're on natural gas or propane, your stove might still work when the power is out. At our previous house we had propane, and our burners still worked but required manual lighting. Our oven didn't work when the electricity was out. At our new cabin, we chose a range that both the burners and oven had a manual light option—no electricity required. Other simple options for cooking might include a camping stove, a camp trailer with a stove and/or oven in it, a barbeque grill, a hibachi, a woodstove, an outdoor fire pit (camp fire), a Sun Oven (or other solar cooker), and canned heat.

If you're using alternative cooking methods, safety is a major concern. If something is designed to be used outside, like a barbeque grill, don't bring it inside to use. Also, be careful of burns.

Does your alternative cooking source require fuel? Be sure to keep propane or charcoal on hand and properly stored.

Depending on the reason for the power outage, you may need to consider conserving fuel or having several cooking sources in case the outage extends beyond your stored fuel. Also, having no-cook foods like nuts and seeds can be a help. Planning for alternative cooking methods early in your pantry stocking journey is a good idea.

Beyond the Pantry

I hope you're now inspired to expand the size of your pantry. The cost-saving and time-saving benefits are well worth the effort. To really help with cost savings, you might wish to take a step beyond the pantry and begin producing your own food in some manner. Producing your own food will take some time, but perhaps not as much as you think. Also, if your pantry stocking efforts have moved more toward food storage, growing or raising your own food would very much compliment those efforts.

There are many "preparedness" websites, books, and articles that talk about storing seeds as part of your food storage system. Some suggest ordering a "tube" of seeds that can be buried in the yard and dug up when times are desperate and a garden is needed as a means for survival. I think having a store of seeds is a terrific idea, but I don't think relying on those buried seeds is a good idea. If you've never gardened before, the time to try it is not when you need to rely on it.

Learning how to grow or raise food during good times is a much smarter way to go about it. You might think you need a considerable amount of space to produce your own food. I've actually been quite surprised during my research on this subject about the amazing things people are doing in minimal surroundings. In this section we'll talk about how you might go about growing your own food right now, no matter what your living circumstances are. This section isn't designed to be a how-to, but rather designed to give you inspiration to think of all the wonderful things you can do to provide food for your family.

The Garden

Probably the first thought everyone has when thinking of growing your own food is having a garden.

One of my favorite books is *Letters of a Woman Homesteader* by Elinore Pruitt Stewart. This book is a collection of actual letters written by Mrs. Stewart when she was homesteading in Wyoming during the early 1900s. Toward the end of the book, she shares how much food she grew for her family for the winter:

> *I never did like to theorize, and so this year I set out to prove that a woman could ranch if she wanted to. We like to grow potatoes on new ground, that is, newly cleared land on which no crop has been grown. Few weeds grow on new land, so it makes less work. So I selected my potato patch, and the man ploughed it, although I could have done that if Clyde would have let me. I cut the potatoes, Jerrine helped, and we*

dropped them in the rows. The man covered them, and that ends the man's part. By that time the garden ground was ready, so I planted the garden. I had almost an acre in vegetables. I irrigated and I cultivated it myself.

We had all the vegetables we could possibly use, and now Jerrine and I have put in our cellar full, and this is what we have: one large bin of potatoes (more than two tons), half a ton of carrots, a large bin of beets, one of turnips, one of onions, one of parsnips, and on the other side of the cellar we have more than one hundred heads of cabbage. I have experimented and found a kind of squash that can be raised here, and that the ripe ones keep well and make good pies; also that the young tender ones make splendid pickles, quite equal to cucumbers. I was glad to stumble on to that, because pickles are hard to manufacture when you have nothing to work with. Now I have plenty. They told me when I came that I could not even raise common beans, but I tried and succeeded. And also I raised lots of green tomatoes, and, as we like them preserved, I made them all up that way. Experimenting along another line, I found that I could make catchup, as delicious as that of tomatoes, of gooseberries. I made it exactly the same as I do the tomatoes and I am delighted. Gooseberries were very fine and very plentiful this year, so I put up a great many. I milked ten cows twice a day all summer; have sold enough butter to pay for a year's supply of flour and gasoline. We use a gasoline lamp. I have raised enough chickens to completely renew my flock, and all we wanted to eat, and have some fryers to go into the winter with. I have enough turkeys for all of our birthdays and holidays.

Reading how much food she needed to put up for winter was a huge eye opener. These days, we don't really think about needing to prepare for winter in the same way. If we run out of food, we can drive to the market and pick up more. We can get anything we want in just about any quantity we desire.

But what if you couldn't get to the store? Are you comfortable with pulling those seeds out of storage (or digging them up) and starting your garden right then?

Our gardening experience since moving to Wyoming has been rather eye opening. When we lived in the Pacific Northwest, it seemed pretty easy to grow things. Some years I did little more than throw some seeds in the ground and they grew. Living in Wyoming has been much more challenging. We're learning to garden completely from scratch in the different climate, with challenging soil and limiting location factors. While we do have a good amount of space for gardening (we live on two acres), there are plenty of other issues. Learning those issues now, when we can enjoy the process, takes a lot of the stress off.

While you might not have, or want, a garden large enough to eliminate the need to go to the market, even a small garden can help with stretching your food budget and providing you with food that you know is grown in a chemical-free manner.

If space is a consideration, there are many methods for high-production gardening in small spaces. Many people are very successful with the square foot gardening method (made famous by Mel Bartholomew) and are able to grow more food in less space.

Along the same lines of square foot gardening is vertical gardening. I've seen some great pictures of gardens growing on walls or fences using minimal space. Some ingenious people even use old gutters and mount them on their house for their vertical garden.

Don't have a yard? Turn your balcony or stoop into a garden with containers. You might be able to combine the container gardening with vertical gardening.

Another great thing we've been learning about is permaculture, sometimes called edible landscaping. This is an interesting process for making all the factors work together. Everything is grown together, either in an organized or haphazard manner, making the "garden" everywhere. For example, instead of planting a row of boxwood as a hedge, you'd plant a row of blueberries. In permaculture you'd choose more native-style plants and develop a system for harvesting rainwater. It's an extremely interesting concept and certainly something worth exploring. Permaculture is said to work in any environment, including in the desert or the high mountains, and in any size space, whether an urban garden or many hundred-acre farm.

Gardening doesn't need to just be a summer activity. In his book *Four Season Harvest*, Eliot Coleman shares how he gardens year around in his Zone 5 Maine garden. Even though the plants aren't actively growing in the dead of winter, he's still harvesting fresh produce.

While this isn't a gardening book, I want to encourage you to at least explore growing some of your own food. You might find gardening to be a wonderful way to stretch your pantry and prepare for an uncertain future, and also a relaxing past time.

Animals

Another great way to extend your pantry is by raising your own meat items. Raising animals can be a wonderful way to control the food you consume, allowing you to know exactly what the animals ate and how they were treated. If you aren't comfortable with the idea of butchering your own food, you might just want to raise a few chickens for eggs.

You don't need to have a farm to raise animals. Many towns and cities allow chickens as long as they're hens only (no roosters). Hens are what you want for eggs, so that works out well. A few chickens are also a great way to process any extra garden greens and kitchen scraps.

If you're comfortable going beyond eggs, those hens also make a wonderful chicken soup after their laying days are over.

Another meat option for small spaces is rabbits. I've had several friends who live in towns that raise rabbits for meat. Rabbits are very quiet and also reproduce fairly easily.

I've even read about people living in cities raising dairy goats for milk and sometimes meat.

Novella Carpenter lives in Oakland, California, and has quite a farm on the vacant lot next to her—chickens, goats, pigs, bees, and more all on a small city space. Her book *Farm City: The Education of an Urban Farmer* was quite interesting (warning: the book contains a considerable amount of profanity). Novella is one of many urban farmers or homesteaders.

Depending on your set up, you could raise a decent amount of meat in a small space. Chickens, ducks, rabbits, goats, sheep, turkey, even fish might all be worth considering. If you have more space, you might consider larger animals such as cattle for meat and/or milk. An additional thing to think about when planning for animals is feeding your animals. Will you grow food for them in your garden? Will you purchase all of their food? If your well-stocked pantry is focused on food storage, putting aside food for animals might be an additional part of that (this includes pets also).

Foraging

You may have heard of foraging. Many people think of foragers as someone wandering around the woods looking for mushrooms (that's what I used to think!), but the definition of foraging is really quite broad: "The acquisition of food by hunting, fishing, or the gathering of plant matter."

Using that definition, we definitely include foraging in our pantry plan. Each fall we strive to fill our freezer with wild game. Living in Wyoming, we have many opportunities for hunting. We also have lots of fishing options. One of my girls absolutely loves fishing, and when the conditions are right, she'll fish several times a week. She likes it so much, she's half owner of a canoe.

The gathering of plant matter is the part of the definition we're very new to. When we lived in the Pacific Northwest, we'd pick wild blackberries almost every year, but until recently, that was the extent of my foraging experience. Now, with the guidance of a friend and the purchase of a book on foraging, we're slowly learning more. I'm excited about this and look forward to how this can add interesting things to our diet.

Sprouts

In the Beans and Legumes section, we talked briefly about sprouting and how using this method of preparation for the beans can make them more digestible. Sprouting is always the perfect way that anyone, anywhere can grow their own food.

Sprouting doesn't take expensive special equipment. It uses very little water and takes minimal time. Sprouts are usually easy to grow, so they're the perfect "plant" if you don't think you have a green thumb. Many things can be sprouted: seeds, nuts, grains, legumes, and grasses.

I've only been sprouting for a few years so have only scratched the surface of sprout options. Sprouts are a super addition to our winter diet when fresh food is out of season and expensive. Sprouting also changes the composition of the seed, nut, legume, grain, etc. and produces a somewhat new item. We already know about the increased digestibility that's induced, but we also get the production of vitamin C and an increase in B vitamins, along with other vitamins and minerals, and even an increase in protein in some sprouts.

Sprouting consists of soaking your seed, grain, etc., and then rinsing them for several days. We do small seeds in a jar with a mesh lid, and larger nuts, legumes, and grains in a colander or sprouting bag (after soaking in a bowl or similar item). Instructions vary slightly depending on what exactly you're sprouting, but it's a very simple process.

We sprout several different types of beans and grains and also keep radish seeds on hand for sprouting. Those little radish sprouts add a wonderful "bite" to a salad or on top of a casserole. You'll definitely want to check out sprouting to keep fresh food in your diet year-round.

Microgreens

Along the same lines of sprouting are microgreens. Microgreens are tiny, edible plants that are grown for up to two weeks. Many of the seeds you'd grow in your outdoor garden can be grown inside as microgreens. Seeds like lettuce, turnips, carrots, sunflowers, and even wheat all make terrific little greens.

You might think microgreens and sprouts are the same, but they're different. Sprouts are grown only in water (soaked and then rinsed), then the entire sprout is cleaned and eaten. With microgreens, the seeds are soaked and then grow in some sort of medium, such as soil. When the sprouts are ready to harvest, this is done by cutting the plant close to the base.

Once you've harvested your microgreens, they can be used in sandwiches, salads, and more. I've even read that microgreens are a high-demand item for upscale restaurants. Microgreens are rather expensive to purchase already grown, but by doing it yourself, you can have these fresh little greens for a lot less. That's definitely one to learn more about.

Indoor Gardening

In addition to little microgreens, you might consider growing full-size plants inside. An indoor vegetable garden doesn't need a ton of space but will need light, either sunlight or special artificial light.

A variety of containers and/or hanging baskets put by a window might be exactly what you need to grow your indoor garden. I've read of people who were able to grow tomatoes, squash, cucumbers, lettuce, and more all by a sunny window.

Another option for an indoor garden is hydroponics. In a nutshell, hydroponics is growing plants without soil, usually in water. There are several variations on the theme of hydroponics, so researching your options and determining what will fit best for your needs, and within your budget, will be important.

When considering an indoor garden, keep in mind that if you have pets, especially cats, they often enjoy green foods too. A few years ago I started a small indoor garden, and one of my cats thought it was all planted just for her. While we didn't get anything from the garden, she enjoyed it immensely.

Regrowing Scraps

This is a gardening concept that I'm brand new to, but I love the sound of it. With this method of gardening, scraps of food that'd normally be tossed in the compost bin are put in water (or sometimes soil), given sunlight, and allowed to regrow.

This concept is said to work well with romaine lettuce, celery, all varieties of onions, and more. The root of the vegetable is saved from the compost bin to be used as a "start" for the new vegetable. I encourage you to learn more about this gardening method and see if it makes sense for you.

Budget Thoughts

Just a few short years ago, we basically had an empty pantry. We moved to Wyoming from the West Coast. The six months before we arrived here, we lived in a twenty-three-foot camp trailer and a fifteen-foot camp trailer. Our house had sold much sooner than expected, so everything we owned needed to fit in the twenty-three-foot trailer (the fifteen-foot trailer didn't move to Wyoming with us) and a 10' x 12' storage unit that we planned to go back and retrieve at a later date. Once we settled in Wyoming, we were on a rather strict budget. We truly started our pantry from scratch—without extra money to put toward it.

In the Beans and Legumes section, we already discussed how adding beans to your pantry and meal plan can help stretch your food dollars. This was just one of the methods we employed to help us make the most of our money and be able to start building up our pantry a little at a time. Cutting down on food waste was also a huge help in cutting our food spending. Here are a few things that worked for us.

Menu Plan

At my house, this is my number one way to help with food waste. My goal is to make a menu plan each Sunday. When

I menu plan, I take inventory of what's in our fridge and needs to be used up first. After the perishables are accounted for, I check the freezer and the pantry. With my method of menu planning, we always "shop at home" first.

While I do find menu planning to be important, also important is remaining flexible. Sometimes I need to alter my menu plan to use up something that magically appeared or that I missed when planning. Reviewing the menu plan for the next day the evening before, plus taking a quick look at your perishables, usually helps with catching these kinds of things. If you notice a few of your apples are starting to get too soft, alter your menu plan to use those up. No one enjoyed last night's squash? Time to alter the menu plan.

Organization

All the menu planning in the world won't get us to the best use of our food dollars if we don't stay organized with the food we prepare. I can rarely predict the exact amount of food my family will consume at each meal. Something needs to be done with the food left over. That's where organization comes in.

What works for me is labeling items as they go in the fridge, then putting them in specific locations. I'm an "out of sight, out of mind" type of person. If a food isn't written on my menu plan but is lurking in my fridge, it had better be where I can see it, or it'll become a science experiment. In the past, I've tried keeping a list on the fridge of things that needed to be used up. While I love that concept, the execution didn't work very well for me. One option is writing leftovers on the menu plan. If you refer to your plan at least one time per day, they'll be in plain sight.

Our main consumption of leftovers occurs as lunches. My husband and daughter often pack leftovers. My little boy and I are usually home at lunchtime, so it's easy to reheat the dish for lunch. I think it's important to point out, I do a lot of planned-overs or Stretchy Meals. Leftovers are a completely different animal than planned-overs. Leftovers are the actual "left over" part of a meal. Those two bowls of chili that didn't get eaten, that serving of casserole—those are leftovers in our house.

Going along with organization is having a plan for things. If you find a great deal on Swiss chard at the farmers market and buy up a case of it, it's no longer a great deal if you only use two bunches and the rest of it rots. Before buying that case, have a plan for using it or preserving it. I often find bananas for twenty-five cents per pound. These are the overripe brown bananas that you probably see in your store often. When these arrive home, they're immediately peeled and put in the freezer. I do leave out a few of the lesser ripe ones for eating. Frozen bananas are perfect for muffins, banana bread, or smoothies.

TV Dinners

Ah...the yummy aroma of a tinfoil-surrounded meal-like substance baking away in the oven. We do sometimes have TV dinners here. But not the kind you're thinking of and that I described. We don't buy those boxed meals; instead, we have our own version. This is a tip I learned from *The Complete Tightwad Gazette* several years ago. When leftovers aren't going to be used up right away, they're packaged up for the freezer. When enough leftovers have accumulated (or when nothing else was planned for dinner), the containers are thawed out and dinner is our own homemade TV dinner smorgasbord extravaganza.

Since we no longer have a microwave, heating up the dishes takes a little time, but it's not at all difficult. I like glass dishes that are freezer safe and oven safe. (You wouldn't want to take them straight from the freezer to a hot oven; those results could be "shattering.") The glass containers are also super easy to label. I write on the glass with a sharpie, and it easily washes off but stays on well in the freezer. Currently, I don't have enough of these glass containers. I do (carefully) use quart jars in the freezer for things like soup or broth. This can be risky if you fill the container to full and it expands. I haven't broken jars, but I've read of others who have. Once again, I label the jar with a sharpie. Once thawed, the soup heats beautifully on the stove top.

While we're in the process of eliminating plastic, we still have some of those plastic storage containers. I'm comfortable with using them in the freezer, but I'm not comfortable with putting hot foods in them. Sometimes, I'll transfer my leftover from a glass container to a plastic one if it's going in the freezer. And then, once the dish is thawed, it's once again transferred to a container for either oven or stove-top cooking, depending on the item. Remember, not everything freezes well. I don't freeze things with potatoes in them since they never thaw well for me (they turn to mush).

Somewhat related to the TV dinner idea is something else learned from *The Complete Tightwad Gazette*: the "soup pot." I keep a container in the freezer for little bits of leftover meats and vegetables. You know when you have two tablespoons of leftover sautéed spinach or 1/4 cup of glazed carrots or a small slice of roast. These items are all put in the soup pot. Once the pot is full, add some of your homemade broth, and you'll have your own version of Stone Soup minus the stone. When you first start with your soup pot, you may wish to keep your flavors similar. We don't mind mixing in Sloppy Joe Beef with Sweet and Sour Chicken, but you might. Of course, you could rinse your meat before putting it in the pot if you wished. Also, your soup pot wouldn't necessarily have to become soup. You could use that wonderful combination of meat and veggies to make a casserole. Keep in mind, you won't have a recipe for creating your soup or casserole out of your soup pot, which is why formula cooking is so important.

Formula Cooking

I love recipes. I love reading cookbooks and looking at food blogs. That said, I rarely follow a recipe as it's written. I look to recipes as being a guide, more than something written in stone. With that thought in mind, many of the dishes we enjoy don't come from a recipe but rather a formula. Once again, this is a concept I learned from *The Complete Tightwad Gazette*. Formula cooking works so well for us that I've shared some of my formulas in my book *Design a Dish*. One of our favorite formula items is muffins. We have muffins often since they're so incredibly versatile and a great way to use up small amounts of surplus items. I really believe that by learning some basic formulas, you can drastically help reduce your food bill and cut down on waste.

Make Something Out of Nothing

We've already somewhat discussed making something out of nothing with our Stone Soup from above. Let's take it a little further. How about making food out of things we'd normally throw away? You may already do this to some degree if you save the ends of your onions for your broth (you do save the ends of your onions to throw in your broth pot, right?) but there are many more things that can be salvaged. In addition to our onion ends, we also keep any bones to use in future broth pots. If we roast a chicken and the bones aren't immediately turned into broth, they're put in the freezer to use later. If instead of a whole roasted chicken we have something with chicken pieces, those bones are also saved for broth. Same with steaks or chops containing bones. I put the bones in freezer bags and label them. I rarely run out of bones for broth by using this method. I understand that this might be a little more than some people wish to do, but it works for us and is, in essence, free food.

Another idea to make something out of nothing includes saving your potato peels and turning them into Potato Skins by tossing them in a combination of olive oil and/or coconut oil and seasonings. Add some shredded cheese and sour cream if you wish for a restaurant-style dish. Or you can use your potato peels for a potassium-rich broth. I've never made it, but I have a (real life) friend who's a Naturopath, and I watched her make it on our local morning show once.

Thinking about how something could be used instead of tossed in the garbage might be a substantial difference in your food bill. I often save lemon halves that I've already juiced in the freezer to put in the cavity of a roasting chicken, as opposed to using a "new" lemon. I also freeze the papers around butter to use for greasing my cookie sheets or baking dishes. These little things can really add up.

Even with these diligent attempts at reducing food waste, there are still going to be some things that can't be salvaged. Instead of tossing those in the garbage, consider composting, vermiposting, or having a few chickens to help with your real food scraps. Our chickens benefit from our real food diet. What they can't have (onions, coffee grounds, etc.) gets composted as future food for our garden.

Keeping food out of the garbage can will help you reduce your food bill. These savings can be put aside and used toward bulk buys. Even saving five to ten dollars each week on your food bill can really add up and help with your pantry filling goals.

Keep in mind, having a well-stocked pantry may have a different meaning for each family. You may be very comfortable having your pantry contain one weeks' worth of meals, or one month. Another person may wish to have three months. Or you may choose to really fill up the pantry and stock twelve months (or more) of food. Set a goal for your family and focus your budget on that goal.

We've discovered that having a well-stocked pantry continues to provide us with cost savings, time savings, and improved health. My hope is that you'll enjoy the same!

More From Millie Copper

Get 20% off Millie Copper's nonfiction eBooks at HomespunOasis.com/Books with coupon code SAVE20.

Stretchy Beans: Nutritious, Economical Meals the Easy Ways

Do you struggle with feeding your family delicious, healthy meals? Are you tired of trying to figure out what's for dinner each night? Do you cringe when you see how much money your family spends on groceries each month?

If so, *Stretchy Beans* is the solution you've been looking for! Learn how to easily prepare dinners that the whole family will love—while staying on budget, spending less time in the kitchen, and not losing your sanity.

Real Food Hits the Road: Budget-Friendly Tips, Ideas, and Recipes for Enjoying Real Food Away from Home

Are you planning to hit the road for a family vacation? Do you want to take a road trip, but the idea of eating out three meals a day doesn't work for your budget or your health?

Real Food Hits the Road will be your guide to saving the budget, keeping your digestion working well, and eating real food away from home while letting you enjoy the trip and not "cook" all of the time.

Design a Dish: Save Your Food Dollars!

Would you like to learn great methods to reduce food waste? What if you could enjoy one meal for "free" each week?

Design a Dish will teach you how to make wonderful, simple dishes you can prepare day in and day out. You'll be amazed at how easy it is to nourish your family with these tasty dishes!

Resources

Find all my favorite resources for real food cooking, homesteading, preparedness, and more at: HomespunOasis.com/resources

Books
The Complete Tightwad Gazette by Amy Dacyczyn
Design a Dish by me, Millie Copper
The Everything Beans Book by Katie Kimball
Nourishing Traditions by Sally Fallon and Mary Enig
Letters of a Woman Homesteader by Elinore Pruitt Steward
Four-Season Harvest by Eliot Coleman
Farm City: The Education of an Urban Farmer by Novella Carpenter

Shopping
Azure Standard (www.azurestandard.com)
Tropical Traditions (www.tropicaltraditions.com)

Education/Information
Weston A. Price Foundation Dietary Guidelines
(http://www.westonaprice.org/basics/dietary-guidelines)
Living With Phytic Acid
(http://www.westonaprice.org/food-features/living-with-phytic-acid)
A Campaign for Real Milk (http://www.realmilk.com/)
Proper Storage Temperatures
(http://www.cde.ca.gov/ls/nu/fd/mb00404.asp)

Putting the Polish on Those Humble Beans (http://www.westonaprice.org/food-features/putting-the-polish-on-those-humble-beans)
Why I No Longer Soak My Beans (http://www.cookingtf.com/why-i-no-longer-soak-my-beans/)
Cooking Dry Beans (http://gnowfglins.com/2006/05/12/cooking-dry-beans/)
13 Week Rotating Menu – featuring Stretchy Beans (https://homespunoasis.com/recipes/13-week-menu-plan/)
The Oiling of America (http://www.westonaprice.org/know-your-fats/the-oiling-of-america)
What Causes Heart Disease? (http://www.westonaprice.org/cardiovascular-disease/what-causes-heart-disease/)
GNOWFGLINS Dehydrating Class (http://gnowfglins.com/ecourse/classes/dehydrate)
GNOWFGLINS Fermenting Class (http://gnowfglins.com/ecourse/classes/ferment)
GNOWFGLINS Sourdough Class (http://gnowfglins.com/ecourse/classes/sourdough)
Backpacking Chef (http://www.backpackingchef.com/)
Sprout People (http://sproutpeople.org/)
FEMA (http://www.ready.gov/) Recommendations for three days of food and water

Recipes
Raw Fudge (http://www.passionatehomemaking.com/2009/12/healthy-homemade-fudge-a-great-gift.html)

Snack Bars (http://gnowfglins.com/2009/12/04/enzyme-rich-homemade-larabar/)

Gingerbread (https://homespunoasis.com/spicy-old-fashioned-gingerbread/)

Muffins (https://homespunoasis.com/design-a-muffin/)

Meet the Author

Millie Copper, writer of Cozy Apocalyptic Fiction, was born in Nebraska but never lived there. Her parents fully embraced wanderlust and moved regularly, giving her an advantage of being from nowhere and everywhere.

As an adult, Millie is fully rooted in a solar-powered home in the wilds of Wyoming with her husband and young son, milking ornery goats and tending chickens on their small homestead. In their free time, they escape to the mountains for a hike or laze along the bank of the river to catch their dinner. Four adult daughters, three sons-in-law, and three grandchildren round out the family.

Since 2009, Millie has authored articles on traditional foods, alternative health, homesteading, and preparedness-many times all within the same piece. Millie has penned five nonfiction, traditional food focused books, sharing how, with a little creativity, anyone can transition to a real foods diet without overwhelming their food budget.

The twelve-installment *Havoc in Wyoming* Christian Post-Apocalyptic fiction series uses her homesteading, off-the-grid, and preparedness lifestyle as a guide. The adventure continues with the *Montana Mayhem* series, scheduled for release in the summer of 2021.

Visit www.HomespunOasis.com for more information, tips, and tricks on budget-friendly real food recipes, homemaking, homesteading, preparedness, and more.

Find Millie at www.MillieCopper.com and www.HomespunOasis.com
Facebook: www.facebook.com/MillieCopperAuthor/
BookBub: https://www.bookbub.com/authors/millie-copper

www.ingramcontent.com/pod-product-compliance
Lightning Source LLC
Chambersburg PA
CBHW020544080526
44583CB00013B/986